Jam Session

Kurt Warner

Terri Dougherty

ABDO Publishing Company

visit us at
www.abdopub.com

Published by ABDO Publishing Company, 4940 Viking Drive, Suite 622, Edina, Minnesota 55435. Copyright © 2000 by Abdo Consulting Group, Inc. International copyrights reserved in all countries. No part of this book may be reproduced in any form without written permission from the publisher.

Printed in the United States.

Cover and Interior Photo credits: AP Wide World Photos; All-Sport Photos

Edited by Denis Dougherty

Sources: Associated Press; Newsweek; New York Daily News; People Magazine; Sports Illustrated; Sports Illustrated For Kids; Time Magazine; ESPN Magazine; USA Today

Library of Congress Cataloging-in-Publication Data

Dougherty, Terri.
    Kurt Warner / Terri Dougherty.
        p.   cm. -- (Jam Session)
    Includes index.
     ISBN 1-57765-426-9 (hardcover)
     ISBN 1-57765-428-5 (paperback)
    1. Warner, Kurt, 1971---Juvenile literature.   2. Football players--United States--Biography--Juvenile literature. 3. St. Louis Rams (Football team)--Juvenile literature. [1. Warner, Kurt, 1971- . 2. Football players.]   I. Title. II. Series.

GV939.W36 D68 2000
796.332'092--dc21
[B]
                                                     00-038611
                                                         CIP
                                                          AC

Contents

Superman to the Rescue

It seemed that Kurt Warner had finally run out of miracles. The story that was too far-fetched for a Hollywood script appeared headed for a heartbreaking climax. Just over two minutes remained in Super Bowl XXXIV on January 30, 2000, at the Georgia Dome in Atlanta. A quarter earlier, it had looked like Kurt's St. Louis Rams were well on their way to completing a dream season with a comfortable Super Bowl victory. But the dream was suddenly in danger of becoming a nightmare. The Rams' 16-0, third-quarter lead had been erased by the hard-charging Tennessee Titans.

A 43-yard field goal by Tennessee's Al Del Greco had tied the score 16-16 with 2:12 left in the game. St. Louis took over at its 27-yard line. Most observers thought the Rams

St. Louis Rams quarterback Kurt Warner.

would play it safe by running the clock out and hoping to pull out a victory in overtime. But Kurt, the league's regular-season Most Valuable Player (MVP), hadn't taken the Rams to the brink of an NFL title by playing it safe.

Ignoring the pain of injured ribs, he thought, "It's time for me to win this game." On the first play, Kurt lofted a bomb down the right sideline just before being leveled by the Titans' ferocious rookie defensive end, Jevon Kearse. Rams wide receiver Isaac Bruce caught the ball at the Tennessee 43-yard line and eluded several defenders on his way to the end zone.

Kurt Warner holds up the Super Bowl trophy after his Rams defeated the Tennessee Titans in Super Bowl XXXIV.

Kurt rose from the ground to see Bruce cross the goal line. He raised his hands in the air. His 73-yard touchdown pass gave St. Louis a 23-16 lead with 1:54 left.

Quarterback Steve McNair led the Titans on one last gutty drive. But when St. Louis linebacker Mike Jones tackled Titans receiver Kevin Dyson one yard short of the goal line, the Rams were Super Bowl champions for the first time. Many called it the best Super Bowl ever.

"I always believed this would happen," Kurt said. "I never gave up. I just worked and worked, and it happened. Now that it has happened, it feels as good as I thought it would."

Kurt, who threw for a Super-Bowl record 414 yards, was the game's MVP. He had completed one of the greatest seasons of any quarterback in NFL history.

His championship-winning pass may have been spectacular, but it was nowhere near as dramatic as the entire Kurt Warner Story: A rags-to-riches sports tale that dwarfed anything film makers could dream up. The story was shocking to everyone except the drama's main character.

Kurt drops back to pass as Jevon Kearse of the Titans applies the pressure.

Passer With Potential

Kurt was born in Burlington, Iowa, and was a tough competitor as a youth. His parents, Gene and Sue, divorced when Kurt was five. His father later remarried, and Kurt lived with his mother in Cedar Rapids, Iowa. He showed promise as a quarterback at Cedar Rapids Regis High School. Tall with a strong arm, he was an all-state selection his senior season.

Kurt was on the football team in college at Northern Iowa, but didn't get a chance to play until he was a senior. That season, he was the Gateway Conference offensive player of the year and led the conference in total offense and passing efficiency. Still, Kurt wasn't chosen in the NFL draft.

He had the chance to go to several training camps, however, and chose the Green Bay Packers. He hoped to earn a spot on the team if another quarterback got injured.

If someone had told then-Packers coach Mike Holmgren he had two future MVP quarterbacks in camp in the summer of 1994, he might have named Brett Favre and either Ty Detmer or Mark Brunell. Favre would win three MVPs and Detmer and Brunell would become starters with other NFL teams. It's doubtful he would have mentioned the shy Warner.

The Packers liked Kurt's talent. But he had a difficult time learning the team's complicated offensive plays. His confidence suffered. When quarterbacks coach Steve Mariucci told him to play during a scrimmage, he said he'd rather stay on the sideline. He didn't think he was ready.

"I felt, from a physical standpoint, I could play," Kurt said. "From a mental standpoint, I felt I had a ways to go, especially after playing only one year in college. I needed to get comfortable with everything I could do and the speed and quickness of the game." Kurt returned to Iowa. His NFL dream would have to wait.

Kurt's first NFL head coach was the Green Bay Packer's Mike Holmgren.

A Star in Another Arena

After the failed tryout with the Packers, Kurt took a night job in a supermarket. For six months, he made minimum wage stocking shelves and bagging groceries at the Hy-Vee in Cedar Falls, Iowa. But he didn't forget football. During the day he worked out and at night he threw rolls of paper towels to co-workers running pass patterns in the aisles.

"That was obviously a very humbling experience," Kurt said. "I was making $5.50 an hour—and I was darn happy to get it. I'd tell the other guys at the store, 'I'll be playing football again someday,' and they'd look at me like I was some guy who just couldn't let it go."

He didn't have a set plan for returning to football until he got a call from Iowa Barnstormers coach John Gregory. The Barnstormers are an Arena Football League team, and play a fast-paced, indoor game. Gregory had watched film of Kurt playing for Northern Iowa, and offered him a chance to play.

In Kurt's first exhibition game, he threw three interceptions and fumbled four snaps. "We only had three or four days to practice before we played," Gregory said. "He was awful, but we were awful, too. The speed of this game is great, and that was his first time."

Kurt improved rapidly. In his first regular-season game, he completed 24 of 35 passes for 285 yards and five touchdowns. Iowa beat Milwaukee 69-61. It was the start of three successful seasons in the Arena League. He averaged 3,400 yards passing and 61 touchdown passes a year.

"He learned to read coverages quickly and throw the ball quickly," Gregory said. "I think he learned to be accurate in our league."

Kurt led Iowa to two straight Arena Bowl appearances. He set all the Barnstormers passing records. His teammates called him "Houdini," after the famous magician. Iowa receiver Kevin Swayne described Kurt this way: "He was a quiet guy, but he had a lot of confidence."

Employees at the Hy-Vee grocery store in Cedar Falls, Iowa, mimic former employee Kurt Warner.

Keeping the Faith

Kurt had a strong Christian faith and a special person to turn to during the ups and downs of his football career. In 1992, he met his future wife, Brenda, at a country music club. She had been in the Marines and was studying to be a nurse.

They were married in 1997. Kurt adopted her children, Zach and Jesse. They have a son, Kade, born in 1998. "The kids mean everything to me," Kurt said. "They are my life."

The family has faced many challenges. In 1996, Brenda's parents were killed when a tornado ripped through their home in Mountain View, Arkansas. Zach had suffered brain damage after falling on his head when he was a baby. He's blind and has trouble learning.

Kurt being congratulated by his wife Brenda after a victory.

"I've had some hard times, but everybody's had some hard times," Kurt said. "And all those things have done is strengthen my character and strengthen me as a person, as well as a player. I don't think I would be the person I am had I not gone through those experiences."

Kurt was happy with his life and his family while he was playing in the Arena League, but still had the dream of being an NFL quarterback. Sometimes he wondered if he would ever make it there.

"I was happy doing what I was doing and content, taking care of my family, but always hoping I would get another opportunity in the NFL—not just a chance to make a team, but to play and show people what I could do," Kurt said.

Kurt with son Kade and wife Brenda.

European Vacation

Soon after Kurt and Brenda got married, it looked as if his NFL dream might come true. Kurt planned to try out with the Chicago Bears after returning from his honeymoon in Jamaica. But one night in Jamaica while Kurt was asleep, a spider bit his elbow. The elbow swelled, and the tryout was canceled.

His next chance came in NFL Europe. Amsterdam Admirals coach Al Luginbill noticed Kurt's success with the Barnstormers and wanted Kurt as his quarterback. But Kurt wanted an American team to sign him before he took the job in Europe, so he would have a better chance of getting into a team's training camp. The Rams agreed to give Kurt a tryout.

At first the tryout looked like another failure. Kurt had played with a broken thumb through half of the Barnstormers' 1997 season. He played well on the small Arena field with the painful injury, but thought it affected his passing during the Rams' tryout.

"I was really frustrated because it was my one chance, and I just wasn't healthy enough to be able to do those things," Kurt said. "I knew that wasn't me out there."

But the Rams were impressed enough to offer him a contract. Kurt signed with the Rams on December 26, 1997, and was the starting quarterback for Amsterdam in 1998. He led the league in passing yards (2,101), attempts (326), completions (165), and touchdowns (15). The Admirals finished the season 7-3.

The next season, Kurt finally had his chance to play in the NFL. He beat out Will Furrer in training camp for the Rams' third quarterback position. He didn't play in the first 14 games of the 1998 season, but moved to the backup position behind Steve Bono after starter Tony Banks injured his knee.

However, he was still playing in obscurity. "No one knew who I was," Kurt said. "I don't think the people in the offices here knew who I was."

Kurt being chased by Detroit Lion's linebacker Allen Aldridge.

Kurt entered his first NFL game in the fourth quarter of the Rams' season finale against the San Francisco 49ers on December 27, 1998. He played three minutes and completed four of 11 passes for 39 yards. He didn't know it then, but that was the beginning of an NFL career that would take him from obscurity to superstardom in one short year.

Passing His First Big Test

By the summer of 1999, Kurt had moved up to the Rams' No. 2 quarterback spot, proving himself in practices. The Rams had been the worst team of the 1990s, and were coming off a 4-12 season. They were picked to finish last in their division.

The team's slim hope for improvement rested with quarterback Trent Green, formerly of the Washington Redskins. Green was off to a great start. But during the team's next-to-last preseason game, Green hurt his knee on a hit from the San Diego Charger's Rodney Harrison. He was out for the season.

The team was devastated. "It was three days around here before anybody could even smile," quarterbacks coach John Ramsdell said.

But Kurt knew he could play at any level if given the chance. "I just felt comfortable out there," Kurt said. "I went out there not thinking that it was a different game than what I had been playing. It was all playing football and making plays. Once they allowed me to just play, it became my team."

Coach Dick Vermeil never considered signing another quarterback. He and the Rams put their faith in Kurt. "Kurt is going to play better than any of the No. 1 draft picks at quarterback this year," Vermeil predicted.

Kurt had only three days of practice with the first team before his first start, in a preseason game against the Detroit Lions. He completed nine of 15 passes for 89 yards in a 17-6 win. "Hopefully, what I did tonight was answer some of those questions," Kurt said.

Kurt runs in for a touchdown.

Not Just a Passing Fancy

*F*ans started to notice Kurt when he threw three touchdown passes in the season opener against the Baltimore Ravens. He became the first NFL quarterback since 1948 to throw three touchdown passes in each of his first three starts.

The team was 3-0 when it faced San Francisco, the NFL's most successful team over the past two decades. The Rams had lost to the 49ers 17 straight times. The Rams took command of the game early, and Kurt passed for 323 yards and five touchdowns in a 42-20 win.

"He's in a zone, and I've never been around anybody who's this hot," Vermeil said after the big win. "A lot of young quarterbacks struggle to adjust to the speed of the game. That's something you can't glean from watching them practice. This kid slows the game down a little bit, and part of that's because of what he went through in the Arena League."

Around the NFL, people were starting to talk about Kurt. He remained confident, and wasn't surprised by his accomplishments. "I've always believed I could be successful," Kurt said. "I've never gone into a situation and thought. 'Well, I can't beat this team out there, I can't perform well.' To say that I'm surprised? I would have to say no."

Kurt, a fundamentalist Christian, pointed to his faith in Jesus when people asked him about his success. Each week, he held a Bible study class in his home. He doesn't smoke, drink, or swear.

"He's a great father, great husband, great friend, and great player—probably in that order," Rams guard Tom Nutten said.

"People are always looking for the secret to my success," Kurt said. "I tell them it's my faith in Jesus Christ. The Lord has something special in mind for this team, and I'm really excited to be a part of it."

Rams coach Dick Vermeil with his starting quarterback Kurt Warner.

Kurt was paid the minimum salary for second-year players. He said any raise he received for the year would be donated to Camp Barnabus, a camp for special needs children and their siblings in Purdy, Missouri.

"Kurt's the most grounded person you'll ever meet," Rams cornerback Todd Lyght said. "Even though he's off the Richter scale right now, there's no way he'll let this go to his head."

The Rams started their season 6-0, and Kurt was a clear choice for MVP. The team then lost close games at Tennessee and at Detroit, but didn't lose again until the meaningless season finale against the Philadelphia Eagles. The Rams finished 13-3 and earned home-field advantage throughout the playoffs.

"This is what I expected to do when I got a chance to play," Kurt said. "I expected to play well and I expected my team to win. And I expect to go a lot farther."

Kurt completed 325 of 499 passes (65.1 percent) for 4,353 yards. He threw only 13 interceptions with 41 touchdown passes, the third-most in NFL history. He led the league with a 109.2 quarterback rating.

"Kurt is an example of what a team player is all about," Vermeil said. "We have an unselfish group of guys and an unselfish leader in Kurt. He has an ego, but it's not big. He simply believes in himself."

Kurt was voted the league's MVP and a Pro Bowl starter. "There were some doubts that I might not get an opportunity to do this," Kurt said. "But there were never any doubts that if I got the opportunity, I could be successful and get to this point."

1999 League MVP Kurt Warner.

Playoff Playmaker

*D*espite everything Kurt and the Rams accomplished in the regular season, doubters remained as the playoffs began. "They haven't beaten a team that finished with a winning record," critics pointed out. "Let's see if this Warner guy can handle the playoff pressure."

In their first playoff game, against the potent Minnesota Vikings, Kurt and the Rams provided the answer. After the Vikings grabbed a 3-0 lead on their opening drive, St. Louis took over at its 23-yard line. On his first play in an NFL playoff game, Kurt threw a 77-yard touchdown pass. He faked a hand-off and threw a perfect pass to Bruce, who caught the ball at the 50-yard line and ran untouched into the end zone.

Fans at the Trans World Dome, where the Rams went unbeaten during the season, rocked the indoor stadium. Kurt went on to complete 27 of 33 passes to 10 receivers for 391 yards and five touchdowns. The Rams won 49-37 and looked forward to hosting the NFC title game.

The Tampa Bay Buccaneers provided a great challenge for Kurt and the Rams. Tampa Bay had one of the best defenses the NFL had seen in years. For more than three quarters, they shut down the Rams. Kurt had thrown three interceptions and had been unable to guide the St. Louis scoring machine into the end zone.

Kurt keeps his cool in his first-ever playoff game.

With just under five minutes left in the game, St. Louis trailed 6-5 and faced a crucial third-and-four play at the Bucs' 30-yard line. Safety Damien Robinson blitzed, and Kurt threw deep down the left sideline to Ricky Proehl. Proehl fended off cornerback Brian Kelly with his right arm and caught the ball against his body with his left. Touchdown!

After stopping Tampa Bay on its last drive, St. Louis had an 11-6 victory and a berth in the Super Bowl. "It's a dream come true," Kurt said. "Everyone who has ever played football has dreamed about playing in a Super Bowl."

Kurt capped his fantastic season with a dramatic Super Bowl victory. But, throughout his rise to stardom, he took the good and the bad one day at a time. "Everybody looks at it from the outside and sees it as this big story," he said. "To me, it's just how it is. Just one day at a time. I lived through the hard times, and now I'm living through the good times.

"You can't really explain it. You can't really put into words what this season has meant," he added. "You just can't describe it. But it's a great feeling, and you try to relish it and enjoy every minute and not get caught up with all the fame and fortune and media. Enjoy it for what it's worth and not make too much out of it."

**Kurt manages to get the pass off despite
being blitzed by Titan's safety Blain Bishop
during Super Bowl XXXIV.**

Kurt Warner Bio

Name: Kurtis Warner

Position: Quarterback

Height: 6-foot-2

Weight: 200 pounds

Birthdate: June 22, 1971

Number: 13

Born: Burlington, Iowa

High School: Cedar Rapids Regis

College: Northern Iowa

Family: wife, Brenda; children, Zachary, Jesse, and Kade

Resides: St. Louis County, Missouri

Personal: Graduated from Northern Iowa with a degree in communications ... lettered in football, basketball, and baseball in high school ... was a Des Moines Register all-state selection in football his senior season ... wears number 13 to prove he's not superstitious ... Started the Iowa Barnstormers' YMCA youth alliance program for at-risk youth. He served as a mentor, spoke at several charity functions, and helped in disciplinary decisions.

Awards and Honors

Gateway Conference Offensive Player of the Year (1993)

First-team All-Arena selection at quarterback (1996 and 1997)

Pete Rozelle Trophy as Super Bowl Most Valuable Player (2000)

Regular-season Most Valuable Player by The Associated Press and Pro Football Weekly/Pro Football Writers Association (1999)

Player of the Year by The Sporting News, Sports Illustrated, Maxwell Club, and Miller Lite (1999)

Pro Bowl starter (2000)

Kurt posing with the Pete Rozelle Trophy (left), and Vince Lombardi Trophy.

Top Five TD Pass Seasons In NFL History

Name	Team	TDs	Year
Dan Marino	Miami	48	1984
Dan Marino	Miami	44	1986
Kurt Warner	**St. Louis**	**41**	**1999**
Brett Favre	Green Bay	39	1996
Brett Favre	Green Bay	38	1995

Top Five QB Rating Seasons In NFL History

Name	Team	Rating	Year
Steve Young	San Francisco	112.8	1994
Joe Montana	San Francisco	112.4	1989
Milt Plum	Cleveland	110.4	1960
Sammy Baugh	Washington	109.9	1945
Kurt Warner	**St. Louis**	**109.2**	**1999**

Top Five Passing Yardage Totals In Super Bowl History

Name	Team	Yards	Year
Kurt Warner	**St. Louis**	**414**	**2000**
Joe Montana	San Francisco	357	1989
Doug Williams	Washington	340	1988
John Elway	Denver	336	1999
Joe Montana	San Francisco	331	1985

Kurt Warner's NFL Postseason Statistics

Opponent	Com.	Att.	Per.	Yds.	TDs	Int.
Minnesota	27	33	81.8	391	5	1
Tampa Bay	26	43	60.5	258	1	3
Tennessee	24	45	53.3	414	2	0

Kurt Warner Chronology

1971 - Born in Burlington, Iowa, on June 22.

1994 - Graduates from Northern Iowa and attends Green Bay Packers training camp.

1995 to 1997 - Quarterback for the Iowa Barnstormers in the Arena Football League.

December 1997 - Signs with the St. Louis Rams.

1998 - Plays for the Amsterdam Admirals in NFL Europe. Joins the Rams as the third-string quarterback.

1999 - Becomes Rams starting quarterback and leads the team to victory in Super Bowl XXXIV. Is the regular season and Super Bowl MVP.

Kurt Warner hands the game ball to a spectator in the crowd.

Glossary

ARENA BOWL - The Arena Football League's championship game.

CONFERENCE - A group of athletic teams that compete against each other on a regular basis.

NFL DRAFT - The National Football League's method of allowing teams to choose players from college teams.

INTERCEPTION - A pass caught by the opposing team.

MVP - Most Valuable Player. The MVP Award is given to the top player in the NFL each season.

QUARTERBACK - Player on offense who calls the signals for the plays. He gets the ball from the center and usually runs, passes, or hands the ball to a running back.

OFFENSE - The team of players on the football field who have control of the ball.

PLAYOFFS - Postseason games played by division winners and wild-card teams to determine a champion.

SCRIMMAGE - A practice game played between two teams.

SUPER BOWL - The National Football League's championship game, played by the champion of the American Football Conference (AFC) and the champion of the National Football Conference (NFC).

TOUCHDOWN - Scoring six points by carrying the ball over an opponent's goal line, or catching, or recovering the ball in an opponent's end zone.

TRAINING CAMP - A series of practices before the football season begins.

Index